WORDS OF WISDOM

OSCAR WILDE

JOLLYJOY

100 Selected Quotes
by Oscar Wilde

Edition 2024

Published by

JOLLYJOY

G/F, 4771/23, Bharat Ram Road, Daryaganj, New Delhi-110002

E-mail: Contact@jollyjoybooks.com

ISBN: 9789363976443

Cover, Typesetting, and Book Design by JollyJoy
Printed & bound in India

ABOUT THE AUTHOR

Oscar Wilde (born October 16, 1854, Dublin, Ireland—died November 30, 1900, Paris, France) was an Irish wit, poet, and dramatist whose reputation rests on his only novel, The Picture of Dorian Gray (1891), and on his comic masterpieces Lady Windermere's Fan (1892) and The Importance of Being Earnest (1895). He was a spokesman for the late 19th-century Aesthetic movement in England, which advocated art for art's sake, and he was the object of celebrated civil and criminal suits involving homosexuality and ending in his imprisonment (1895–97).

100 SELECTED QUOTES

"To live is the rarest thing in the world.
Most people exist,
that is all."

"Be yourself;

everyone else is already taken."

"We are all in the gutter,
but some of us are looking at the stars."

*"Every saint has a past,
and every sinner has a future."*

*"Always forgive your enemies;
nothing annoys them so much."*

"Never love anyone who treats you like you're ordinary."

"I am so clever that sometimes I don't understand a single word of what I am saying."

YOU
CAN
NEVER
BE
OVERDRESSED
OR
OVEREDUCATED

THE
TRUTH
IS
RARELY
PURE
AND
NEVER
SIMPLE

*"Women are meant to be loved,
not to be understood."*

"An idea that is not dangerous
is unworthy of being called an idea at all."

A
GOOD
FRIEND
WILL
ALWAYS
STAB
YOU
IN
THE
FRONT

"Death must be so beautiful.
To lie in the soft brown earth,
with the grasses waving above one's head,
and listen to silence.
To have no yesterday,
and no tomorrow.
To forget time,
to forgive life,
to be at peace."

"We are each our own devil,
and we make this world our hell."

"Live! Live the wonderful life that is in you!
Let nothing be lost upon you.
Be always searching for new sensations.
Be afraid of nothing."

"I have the simplest tastes. I am always satisfied with the best."

"I don't want to go to heaven.
None of my friends are there."

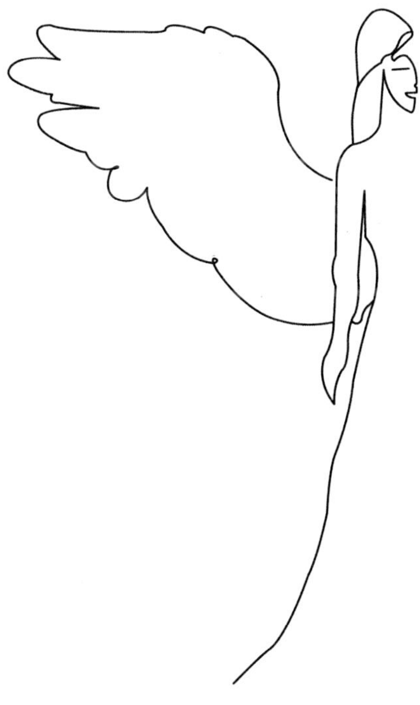

"I am not young enough to know everything."

*"If one cannot enjoy reading a book
over and over again,
there is no use in reading it at all."*

"I have nothing to declare except my genius."

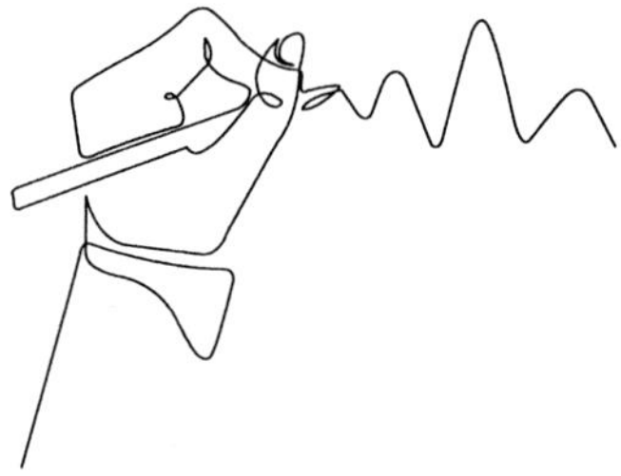

NO GOOD DEED GOES UNPUNISHED

"Life is far too important a thing ever to talk seriously about."

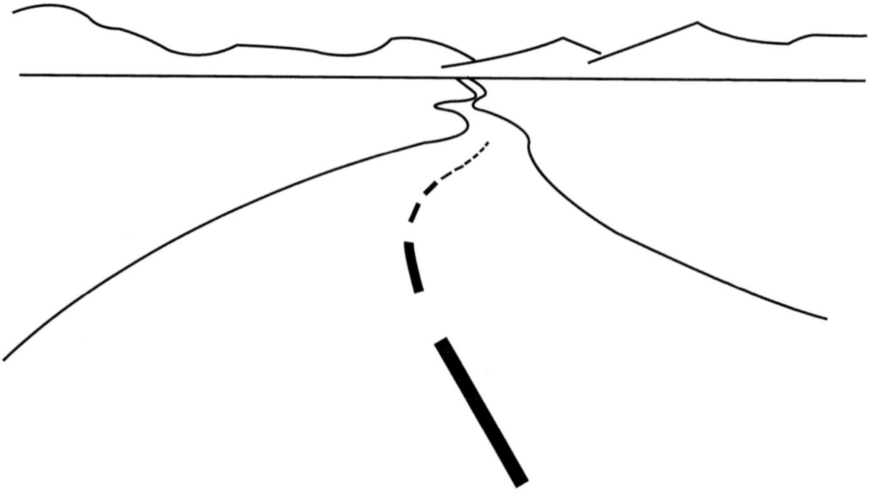

"Experience is merely the name men gave to their mistakes."

"The best way to appreciate your job is to imagine yourself without one."

"The heart was made to be broken."

"It is what you read when you don't have to that determines what you will be when you can't help it."

"Man is least himself when he talks in his own person.
Give him a mask,
and he will tell you the truth."

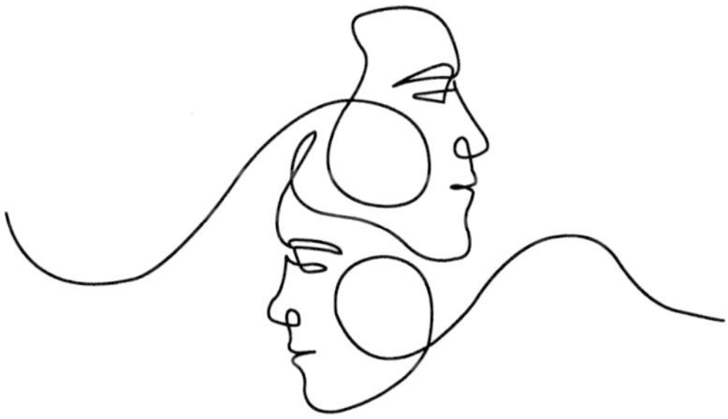

*"Anybody can sympathise with
the sufferings of a friend,
but it requires a very fine nature to
sympathise with a friend's success."*

"The books that the world calls immoral are books that show the world its own shame."

"Hear no evil,
speak no evil,
and you'll never be invited to a party."

"A bore is someone who deprives you of solitude without providing you with company."

"Anyone who lives within their means suffers from a lack of imagination."

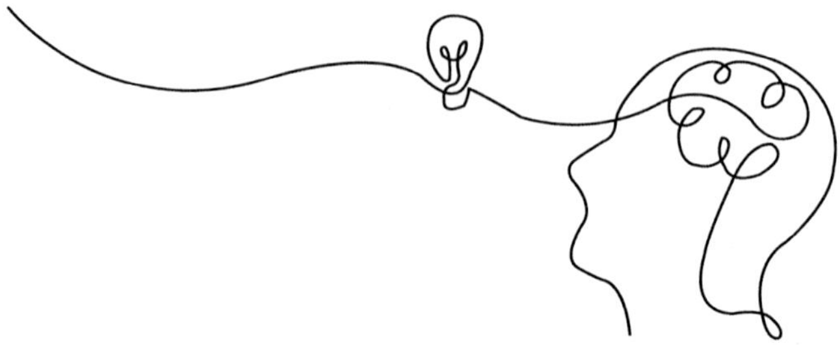

*"You don't love someone for their looks,
or their clothes, or for their fancy car,
but because they sing a song only you can hear."*

"Fashion is a form of ugliness so intolerable that we have to alter it every six months."

"A dreamer is one who can only find his way by moonlight, and his punishment is that he sees the dawn before the rest of the world."

*"Some cause happiness wherever they go;
others whenever they go."*

"Most people are other people.
Their thoughts are someone else's opinions,
their lives a mimicry,
their passions a quotation."

*"Men marry because they are tired;
women, because they are curious:
both are disappointed."*

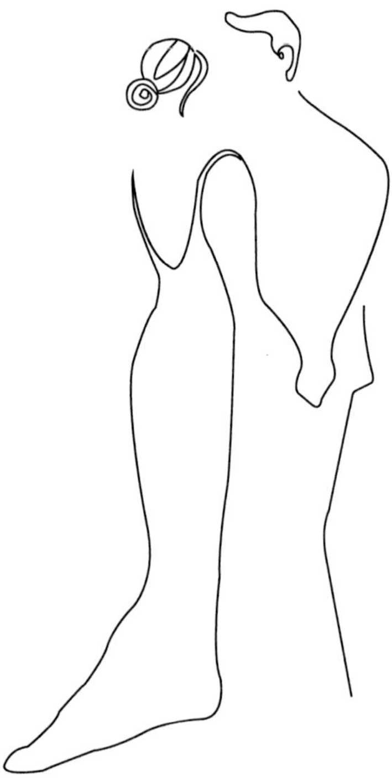

QUOTATION
IS
A
SERVICEABLE
SUBSTITUTE
FOR
WIT

NO
MAN
IS
RICH
ENOUGH
TO
BUY
BACK
HIS
PAST

"Education is an admirable thing,
but it is well to remember from time to time that
nothing that is worth knowing can be taught."

"If you cannot write well,
you cannot think well;
if you cannot think well,
others will do your thinking for you."

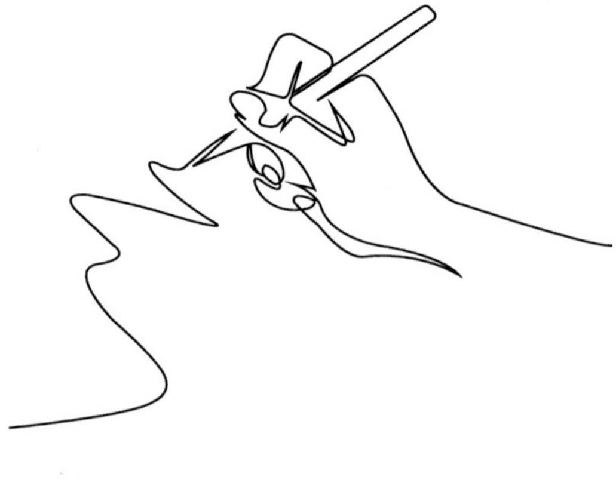

TO

DEFINE

IS

TO

LIMIT

"Whenever people agree with me
I always feel I must be wrong."

“Life is not complex.
We are complex.
Life is simple,
and the simple thing
is the right thing.”

"The old believe everything,
the middle-aged suspect everything,
the young know everything."

"Everything in the world is about sex except sex.
Sex is about power."

"Never regret thy fall,
O Icarus of the fearless flight For the greatest
tragedy of them all Is never to feel the burning light."

*"You will always be fond of me.
I represent to you all the sins you never
had the courage to commit."*

"I am too fond of reading books to care to write them."

"Society often forgives the criminal;
it never forgives the dreamer."

"Imitation is the sincerest form of flattery that mediocrity can pay to greatness."

THE
VERY
ESSENCE
OF
ROMANCE
IS
UNCERTAINTY

"A man who does not think for himself does not think at all."

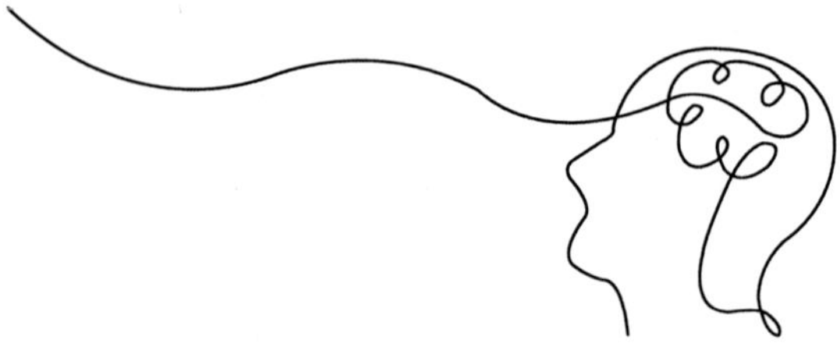

"I beg your pardon I didn't recognise you –
I've changed a lot."

*"Selfishness is not living as one wishes to live,
it is asking others to live as one wishes to live."*

"How can a woman be expected to be happy with a man who insists on treating her as if she were a perfectly normal human being."

"Life has been your art.
You have set yourself to music.
Your days are your sonnets."

"A passion for pleasure is the secret of remaining young."

"A writer is someone who has taught his mind to misbehave."

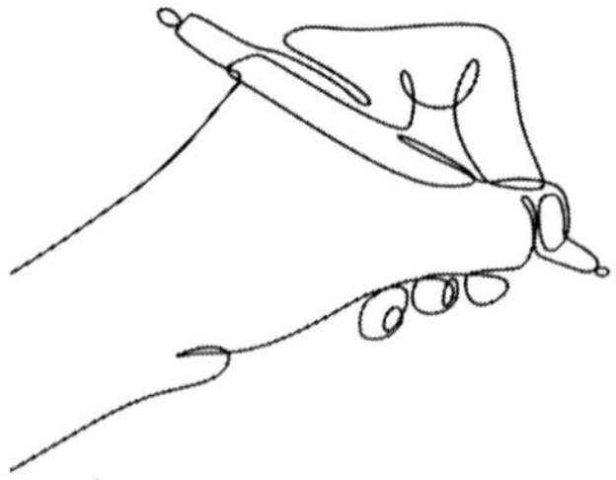

"Ordinary riches can be stolen,
real riches cannot.
In your soul are infinitely precious things that cannot be taken from you."

"Keep love in your heart.
A life without it is like a sunless garden
when the flowers are dead.
The consciousness of loving and being loved brings a
warmth and a richness to life that nothing else can bring."

"Behind every exquisite thing that existed, there was something tragic."

"There are moments when one has to choose between living one's own life, fully, entirely, completely-or dragging out some false, shallow, degrading existence that the world in its hypocrisy demands."

"For one moment our lives met,
our souls touched."

EVERY WOMAN IS A REBEL

*"If you don't get everything you want,
think of the things you don't get that you don't want."*

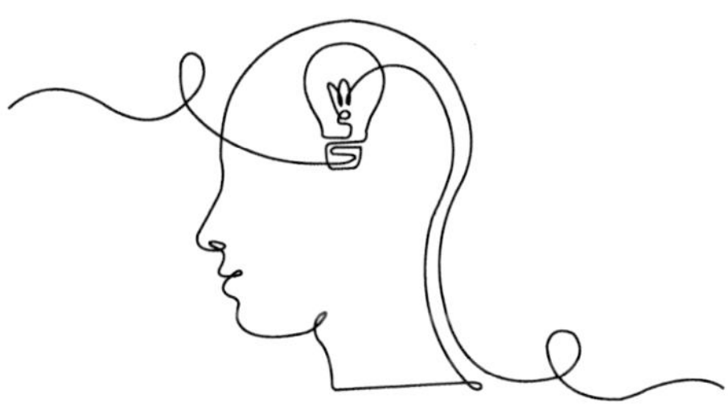

"Democracy means simply the bludgeoning of the people by the people for the people."

"I never travel without my diary.
One should always have something sensational
to read in the train."

"A little sincerity is a dangerous thing,
and a great deal of it is absolutely fatal."

*"Man is many things,
but he is not rational."*

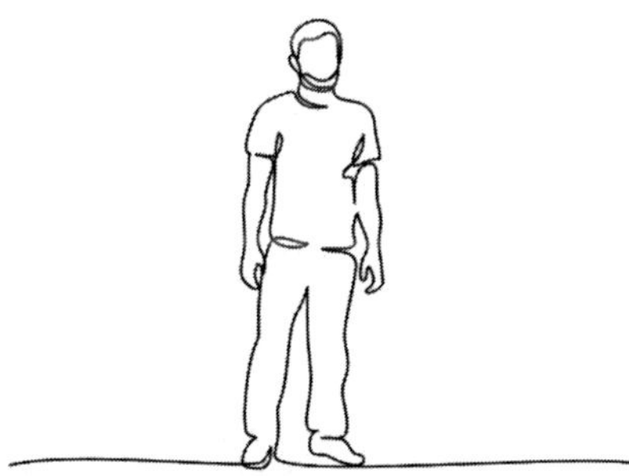

"The basis of optimism is sheer terror."

PATRIOTISM
IS
THE
VIRTUE
OF
THE
VICIOUS

TO
BE
POPULAR
ONE
MUST
BE
A
MEDIOCRITY

*"To regret one's own experiences is to arrest
one's own development.
To deny one's own experiences is to put
a lie into the lips of one's own life.
It is no less than a denial of the soul."*

"It is through art,
and through art only,
that we can realise our perfection."

"I knew nothing but shadows and
I thought them to be real."

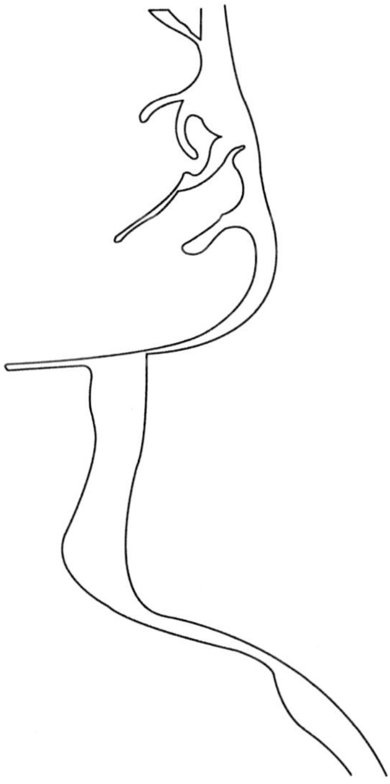

"I like talking to a brick wall- it's the only thing in the world that never contradicts me!"

"Arguments are to be avoided,
they are always vulgar and often convincing."

"I like men who have a future and women who have a past."

"And what sort of lives do these people,
who pose as being moral,
lead themselves?
My dear fellow,
you forget that we are in the native
land of the hypocrite."

"When I like people immensely
I never tell their names to anyone.
It is like surrendering a part of them.
I have grown to love secrecy."

"Humanity takes itself too seriously.
It is the world's original sin.
If the cave-man had known how to laugh,
History would have been different."

"One's real life is so often the life not lead."

"He wanted to be where no one would know who he was.
He wanted to escape from himself."

"I never put off till tomorrow what I can possibly do – the day after."

*"A cynic is a man who knows the price of everything,
and the value of nothing."*

*"There is no such thing as a moral or an immoral book.
Books are well written,
or badly written.
That is all."*

"To love oneself is the beginning of a lifelong romance."

"When a woman marries again,
it is because she detested her first husband.
When a man marries again,
it is because he adored his first wife.
Women try their luck; men risk theirs."

"The most terrible thing about it is not that it breaks one's heart – hearts are made to be broken – but that it turns one's heart to stone."

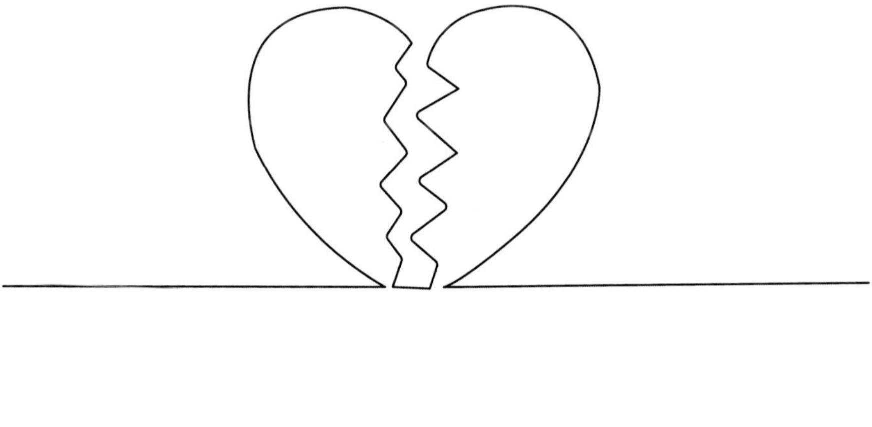

"People who count their chickens before they are hatched act very wisely because chickens run about so absurdly that it's impossible to count them accurately."

"This wallpaper is dreadful,
one of us will have to go."

"There are only two tragedies in life:
one is not getting what one wants,
and the other is getting it."

"In old days books were written by men of letters and read by the public. Nowadays books are written by the public and read by nobody."

"Sin is a thing that writes itself across a man's face. It cannot be concealed."

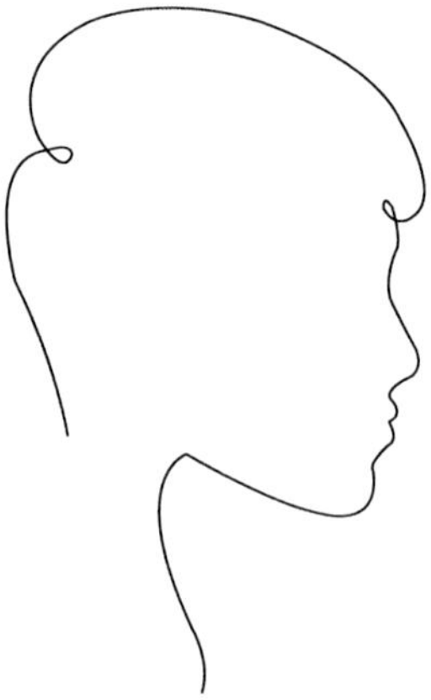

"The smallest act of kindness is worth more than the grandest intention."

"One should never trust a woman who tells one her real age.
A woman who would tell one that would tell one anything."

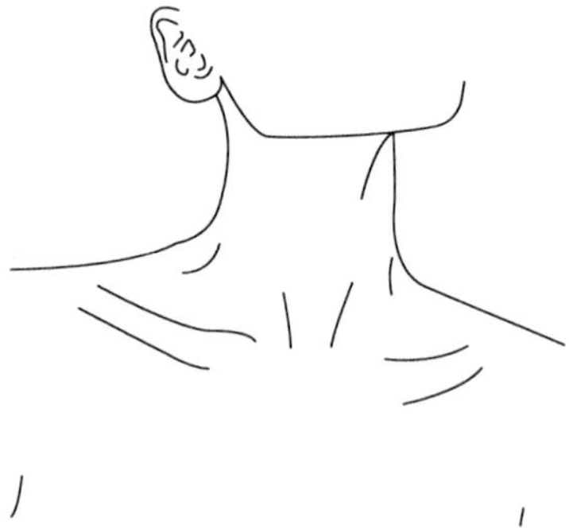

"Everything in moderation, including moderation."

"Being natural is simply a pose,
and the most irritating pose I know."

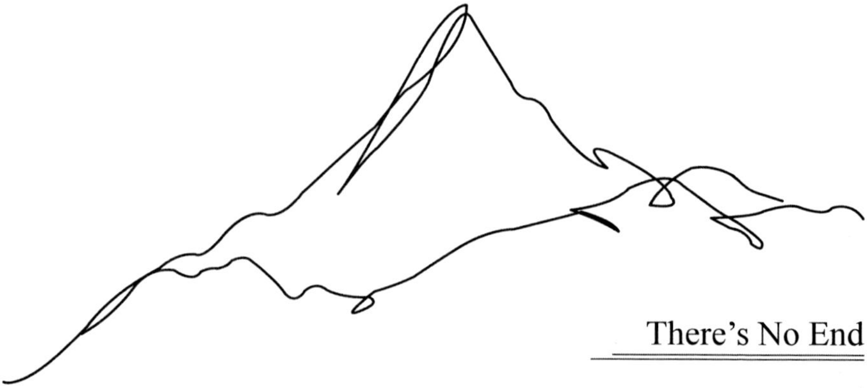